Alistair has managed to
Testament pass
Christ in chapter
making this book
Bible time or gift for

Linda Allcock, autho ... er,
London Seminary

One of the reasons our world is tearing itself apart is that it has rejected and lost sight of the story of God. Road Map to Jesus *simply makes you love the beautiful story more and marvel at its Author. Like a masterful detective, Alistair Chalmers has done a brilliant job of pulling together the threads that reveal Christ in the Old and New Testaments. As a church we desperately need to be captivated afresh with the whole Biblical narrative and communicate it to a world that has never needed it more. I am excited by the potential this book has to do this.*

Phil Knox, Evangelical Alliance and author of *Story Bearer* and *The Best of Friends*

Enlightening, exciting and easy to read, Road Map to Jesus *places us with the disciples on the Emmaus Road journeying through the bigger story of the Bible and how it all points to our glorious saviour. In these short chapters, Alistair Chalmers makes the riches of the Old Testament easy to digest and accessible to anyone, leaving us asking our own response to Jesus and his word. This book helped me make connections I had never before seen, giving a richer and deeper view of who Jesus is, that He is the same yesterday, today and forever. I would recommend to anyone wanting to see Jesus in all the pages of scripture!*

Abi Andrews, Staff Worker, UCCF

Road Map to Jesus *is a clear and helpful resource for those desiring to see the connection between Jesus and the Old Testament. This book connects many Old Testament passages to the person and work of Jesus and shows how Jesus fulfills those hopes and promises. Anyone wanting to grow in their understanding of Jesus and the Old Testament will find this a helpful guide and useful resource. This book is an excellent introduction to some key Old Testament passages and prophecies.*

Dustin Greenup, youth pastor, Indian Trail Church

ROAD MAP TO JESUS

ROAD MAP TO JESUS

ALISTAIR CHALMERS

10 Publishing
a division of 10ofthose.com

First published in Great Britain in 2023

British Library Cataloguing in Publication Data
A record for this book is available from the British Library

ISBN: 978-1-913896-82-9

Designed and typeset by Pete Barnsley (CreativeHoot.com)

Printed in Denmark

10Publishing, a division of 10ofthose.com
Unit C, Tomlinson Road, Leyland, PR25 2DY, England

Email: info@10ofthose.com
Website: www.10ofthose.com

1 3 5 7 10 8 6 4 2

To my wife, Sabine,
who has been the best companion and
support on my journey of getting to
know Jesus more

CONTENTS

INTRODUCTION

Many people find the Old Testament uncomfortable. It's treated a little bit like the New Testament's strange, older cousin. To our modern, *enlightened* minds, what the Old Testament describes is outdated at best and primitive at worst – at least, that's often how it's portrayed.

And yet when Jesus – on the very same day that he rose from the dead – wanted to explain his mission and purpose to two of his friends, he chose to use words from the very same Old Testament (Luke 24:13–35).

There is nothing more important than knowing and understanding Jesus. He's often thought of as a good guy or a moral teacher, or even as a political and social activist. But it is only by looking at the Old Testament that we can see that he is so much more.

Do you think the Old Testament is irrelevant? Are you overwhelmed by its size? Do you wonder why it makes up so much of the Bible?

My hope is that this book will answer these questions, showing that the Old Testament exists to teach us about who Jesus is and what he came to do. In other words, as we journey through the Old Testament, we'll see how it's a road map to Jesus.

Regardless of how you come to this book, I want you to be challenged and encouraged. Most importantly, I want to point you to Jesus so you can see how wonderful he is.

PART 1:

A PATHWAY THROUGH THE OLD TESTAMENT

1

SETTING THE STAGE

And beginning with Moses and all the Prophets, he explained to them what was said in all the Scriptures concerning himself. (Luke 24:27)

The Bible is a big book that has lots to say about Jesus, so the question is where do we start? As I've journeyed through the Christian life, one of the passages that has always intrigued me is Luke 24:13–35. Let me give you a quick summary.

Just after Jesus' crucifixion, all of his followers dispersed including the disciples who had been with him for three years. They were afraid that they could meet the same death if they were to stick around. Some locked themselves in an upper room of a building. Two others decided to walk to Emmaus, which is about seven miles from Jerusalem, where Jesus was crucified.

What those followers on the road to Emmaus didn't know is that Jesus had been resurrected – God had brought him back from the dead. As they walked along the road, the Bible tells us that they were discussing everything that had happened. I'm sure they were remembering the miracles they'd seen Jesus perform and his powerful teaching to the crowds. But I'm also sure that they were discussing how difficult and confusing it was that their friend and teacher was now dead. They would have been terrified, hurt, discouraged and lonely. The man they had trusted and believed in was suddenly gone, having been branded a criminal and executed despite having done nothing wrong.

As they walk, the resurrected Jesus joins them on their journey, but the Bible also tells us that they are kept from recognising him. Coming alongside them, Jesus asks what they're talking about and what's been going on in Jerusalem of late. One of the followers, a man named Cleopas, speaks up and tells him everything that has happened. Cleopas explains who they thought Jesus was and how he had been crucified, but that, strangely, some of their friends went to his tomb that morning and found it empty. Jesus' body was gone.

Jesus asks them, and I paraphrase, 'Isn't that what you were expecting? The prophets (God's messengers in the Old Testament) said that the sent one from God must suffer before his glory.' He then began to explain to them, from the Old Testament, what was foretold about him.

I've read that passage so many times since becoming a Christian, and every time I have thought that I would love to have been a fly on the wall in that Bible study! Cleopas and his friend needed to be reminded of, or maybe to understand properly for the first time, who Jesus really was. If we're honest, we need that too.

While the Bible doesn't tell us exactly which Old Testament passages Jesus spoke about, there are plenty of key sections he could have chosen. We're going to walk through some of them and see how the Old Testament points us to Jesus, helping us to understand who he is and what he did for the world while on earth.

The Old Testament is a treasure chest that points to Jesus as the Son of God who came to earth in human flesh. His purpose was to reconcile people to God and to restore their broken relationship. To know how that was possible, let's follow the map and journey together.

2

POWERFUL WORDS

> *In the beginning God created the heavens and the earth. Now the earth was formless and empty, darkness was over the surface of the deep, and the Spirit of God was hovering over the waters.*
>
> *And God said, 'Let there be light,' and there was light.* (Genesis 1:1–3)

Words are powerful. The words used to describe us can either encourage or hurt. The way we are spoken to and spoken of can have a big impact on how our day goes and sometimes affect our future. However, our words do not have authority or power in the sense that we can control all things or create with our words. Right at the beginning of the Bible is the story of creation. The book of Genesis talks about the creation of the world, including light, animals and humanity. But the main thing that it communicates is that God is great and powerful. In Genesis 1, the repeated refrain is that God said and it happened. Unlike us, God can speak things into being. His words are all-powerful and his control is absolute.

So as Jesus is walking down the road to Emmaus and explaining who he is, imagine how the two followers would have felt when they realised that they were in the presence of this God during his earthly ministry. But it shouldn't have been news to them really, because some of Jesus' followers and disciples had seen the power of his words before and surely would have told Cleopas and his friend all about it.

In Mark 4:35–41, Jesus and his 12 disciples are on a boat when there is a big storm. The waves crash against the boat and the seasoned fishermen are afraid, thinking that they are dying. All this time, Jesus is asleep. Out of fear, the disciples wake him up and ask Jesus whether he doesn't care if they die. Jesus gets up and commands the waves with his words: 'Quiet! Be still' (verse 39).

In that moment, the disciples get a glimpse of who they are following. Jesus is not just another man. Jesus is not just a great teacher who has started to gain popularity. As time goes on, the disciples would see more and more of who Jesus really is and that his words are powerful. In Mark 4–5 alone, we see that Jesus has power over creation, evil, illness and death. In each case, Jesus proves his power by the power of his words. He spoke and it happened.

Maybe you're reading this book because you too aren't sure what you make of Jesus yet. Maybe you've picked it up because you want to learn more about him or because you want to meet him for the first time. As we go on this journey together, we will see not only who Jesus is and what he did, but also how he continues to work in and through people today. Genesis, the beginning of the Bible, is just the beginning of the story. The end of the story is glorious.

Genesis speaks of a powerful and awesome God. In Jesus, we see that same God taking on flesh and becoming one of us. Jesus did so in order that we could know God and join his family. He gives us the opportunity to live the lives that we were created to live. Jesus has all authority and power. The starting point of your journey is to see that the same all-powerful one who spoke the world into being and who calmed the waves some two thousand years ago is the same one who is calling you to consider for yourself who he is, maybe for the first time. He wants you to grow in your knowledge and love for him.

3

GOD'S PRESENCE

> *Then the man and his wife heard the sound of the* Lord *God as he was walking in the garden in the cool of the day, and they hid from the* Lord *God among the trees of the garden. But the* Lord *God called to the man, 'Where are you?'* (Genesis 3:8–9)

Being around your loved ones is important. Christmas may be one of those times when you gather with the whole family and enjoy each other's company. You spend time talking, eating, walking and having a laugh together. Time with all those we love, whether friends or family, is valuable.

The glorious picture that the Bible presents is that Adam and Eve spent time in the presence of God. God created Adam and Eve, made them his image bearers, gave them a beautiful garden to look after and was present, walking and talking, with them.

As we'll see later on, that presence was interrupted, in a big and disastrous way. But it was more serious than just a family argument over Christmas. It was more serious than the pain of being far away from friends or family. The presence of God with Adam and Eve was broken completely. While God did promise that this wasn't the end of the story, the reality of restoration was a long way off for Adam and Eve personally.

Throughout the Bible, we see specific moments when God is present again with his people. There are moments of reconciliation, but it's never the same as the presence that we read about in the beginning of the Bible. Something needs to change for that presence to be properly restored.

We see the beginnings of that restoration in Jesus. He comes into the world, God in the flesh, and dwells with people. Jesus journeys with people and spends time with them. This is not only with the easy people or the people who were like him – Jesus spends time with all kinds of people. He tells them about the kingdom of God – a place where the presence of God will be with his people again. However, this will not be in the same way as it was in Eden. In the kingdom of God, his presence will be far greater than we can ever imagine and it will be forever.

Jesus, being God in the flesh, was the only one who was able to completely restore the broken relationship between humanity and God. In the Garden of Eden, God was present with Adam and Eve, but that was destroyed because they rebelled against him. However, we are told that, in the kingdom of God, he will dwell with his people and wipe away their tears (Revelation 21:1–4). In God's eternal kingdom, there will be no more pain, suffering or death. God will be in perfect harmony with his people and there will be no end to that. The Bible begins with the story of how peace between God and humanity was broken. The Bible ends with the promise of this relationship being completely restored. Jesus stands in the middle as the one who makes that possible. Only through Jesus can sinful, rebellious people be at peace with God.

We may look forward to spending time with family and friends that we haven't seen for a while. We will prepare for and look forward to that day with excitement and anticipation, but sooner or later our time visiting loved ones comes to an end. The promise of God's presence, through Jesus, is that God will dwell with his people permanently. We can know God's presence now, but the fullness of it is yet to come. What a day it will be when God's presence is restored!

4

SIN

And the LORD *God commanded the man, 'You are free to eat from any tree in the garden; but you must not eat from the tree of the knowledge of good and evil, for when you eat from it you will certainly die.'* (Genesis 2:16–17)

There is a point in everyone's life where they push the boundaries and break the rules. You don't need to teach a toddler to say no. It's as if we're born with that word already in our vocabulary. We have a natural desire to disobey anyone who says we can't do a certain thing. We want to rebel. Children don't want to listen to parents when they're told to play nicely and share their toys. Teenagers don't want to listen when they're told to be back before dark. Drivers don't want to keep the speed limit – it just doesn't seem to get you there quick enough. All of these things are different from the perfect world we see at the beginning of the Bible. What changed?

The Bible begins with a beautiful picture of Adam and Eve living in harmony with God. They are given authority to rule over the Garden of Eden and all the living things. They only have one rule to follow: they aren't allowed to eat from the tree in the middle of the garden. But the snake tempts Adam and Eve into sin by putting the seed of doubt in their minds. He questions, 'Did God really say?' (Genesis 3:1). The serpent continues by telling Adam and Eve that God doesn't want them to be like him, knowing good and evil. And so first Eve and then Adam eat fruit from the forbidden tree.

Sadly, this first rebellion against God is not an isolated event; its effects live on in the heart of every human being today. Because of this first wrong, the rest of humanity has been infected with the same fatal disease: sin. There is no escaping this disease. No one is exempt from it. This is why we don't like following rules. This is why it's so easy for us to lie. Sin is the reason that we are all, by default, enemies of God who deserve to be punished for our rebellion.

But the story doesn't stop there, as we'll see as we journey this road together. There was one man who was without sin. The whole of the Old Testament points forward to him and teaches the people of Israel about his coming. They knew him as the Messiah; we know him as Jesus.

Jesus was not a moral teacher. He was not just a good person who did nice things to those around him. Jesus was the only person to have ever lived without committing any sin. He was able to fully obey God's commandments because he was God in the flesh. At the same time, Jesus understands what we are like because he is also fully human. He is both fully God, so could withstand the temptations in our world, and fully man, so can sympathise with humanity and know our struggles. And the good news doesn't stop there.

Jesus came to earth not just to live a sinless life but also to make a way for a sinful people to be reconciled with a perfect God. Our rejection of God has broken our relationship with him. There is a big void between the created and our Creator. But Jesus, being fully God and fully man, has made it possible for our sin to be forgiven.

The Bible begins with a garden where Adam and Eve live in harmony with God, but the Bible ends in a greater garden where the Lord will dwell with his people forever (Revelation 22:1–5). Though sin prevents us from entering into that first garden, Jesus came to break the power of sin and has enabled people to be made right with God again so we can look forward to being with him in the greater garden.

5

JUDGMENT

So the L*ORD* *God said to the snake, 'Because you have done this, cursed are you …'* (Genesis 3:14)

Judgment. When you hear that word, you might think of a person sitting in a raised seat, wearing a white wig and black gown, and holding a little hammer, eager to hand out harsh punishments. The same can often be true when we think of God and judgment. Maybe you imagine God rubbing his hands together, eager to bring down severe judgments and punishments on the world. But that's not what we see in the Bible at all.

The first judgment occurs in the book of Genesis. Adam and Eve have rejected God, and instead believed the lie of the snake. They have eaten the forbidden fruit in disobedience to God. As God is just, he must punish their sin. For every sin there is a consequence. Previously, Adam and Eve lived in perfect harmony with God in the Garden of Eden, enjoying his presence and their work in caring for God's creation. But after they rebel against and reject God, their lives – and the rest of the world – will never be the same again. God banishes Adam and Eve from the Garden of Eden and forbids them to enter ever again. Because of their sin, the earth is cursed. In addition, God declares that work will become tiresome and that childbearing will become painful and hard.

Life as we know it is not actually the way it was supposed to be. As a result of sin, judgment has come upon the world and on the human heart. This judgment doesn't only affect humanity; it has damaging effects on the whole of creation. Our desires are no longer for the things of God, but for our own fame and glory. Our relationships with each other are marked by friction or worse. Our work isn't always fruitful or fun, but can be hard and discouraging. Our bodies are not always the pinnacle of health, and we suffer the almost constant deterioration of the human anatomy before death comes to us all.

These judgments have become normal to us. We experience hardship and ill-health. We experience a broken creation and know that death is the end that awaits every living thing. The curses in Genesis 3 are in full effect today. Every mother will tell you that the pains of giving birth are still very real. Every worker will tell you of the frustrations that they face. Every gardener will tell you how annoying weeds are.

One of the curses in Genesis 3 is that the ground will produce thorns (verse 18). This might sound like an insignificant detail to skip over and forget. However, the thorns represent hardship and pain, struggle and sin. And before we grumble at the judgments that we have been given, we must remember that no one is innocent.

Even more importantly, we need to be thankful that judgment doesn't have to have the final word. If we fast forward in time to John's Gospel in the New Testament, we read of a crown of thorns that is put on Jesus' head. Soldiers mock and beat Jesus, an innocent man who has been sentenced to death. Along with the crown of thorns they make him wear, they put a purple robe on his body and make fun of him, saying, 'Hail, king of the Jews!' (John 19:3).

Little did they know that before them *was* the King of the universe – Jesus is not only King of the Jews. He is the King for whom and through whom all things were created and the one who holds all things together (Colossians 1:16–17). The crown that they use to mock Jesus points to the wonderful truth that he is the King who bore the sin and curses of the world on the cross. The cross of Jesus is not a place of defeat; it is not a tragic death; it is not the end. Jesus rose again from the dead, proving that neither his death nor our sin and judgment have the final say. Life and forgiveness can be found in the King who laid down his life so that whoever believes in him will have eternal life.

6

SALVATION PROMISED

And I will put enmity
between you [the snake] and the woman,
and between your offspring and hers;
he will crush your head,
and you will strike his heel. (Genesis 3:15)

We love stories that have happy endings. Hollywood is built on the concept of hope in times of despair. You'll know this if you've ever seen a movie with a battle scene. The fight is the darkest moment, with despair and horror all around, but on the horizon comes the glimmer of hope: reinforcements. We all want hope in the darkest of times. We want to see the sun shining through the storm clouds. Such storylines find their beginnings not in the minds of film directors or scriptwriters, but in the beginning of the Bible.

Genesis 3 is known for God's judgment and his curses on the snake, Eve, Adam and the world. It's the chapter that people don't like, but it explains our struggles so well – struggles of life, of work, of relationships and of death. Also, in the midst of the bad news and the judgment of sin, this chapter is where we hear about the best news this world has ever known.

Sin took root in Adam's and Eve's hearts because they believed the lies of the serpent. They believed that the forbidden fruit would make them like God, knowing both good and evil. However, in Genesis 3:15, we read that God tells the snake that one of Eve's offspring 'will crush your head'. The wonderful news is that one day the snake crusher will come. This man will deal with the consequences of the serpent's actions and stop the damage of sin.

In the middle of God's pronouncements of the consequences of sin, hope is found in the offspring of a woman. He will give the death blow to humanity's enemy. This is light shining in the storm, hope in despair. But there will be a cost: 'he will crush your head, and you will strike his heel'. This man will crush the snake's head, but he will be hurt in the process.

Because of our place in history, we know that this serpent crusher is Jesus. He came as one of us, born of a woman, into our sin-stained world. But he was different. He wasn't under the curse of the rest of humanity – Jesus is fully God and fully man. His identity meant that only he could be the one to end the effects of the snake. Only he could deal the final blow that would destroy the damage that the serpent had put in motion.

The promise of the serpent crusher is the best news that the world has ever known because without Jesus and his work, we would still be under the full consequences of sin. While we will always feel the effects of sin while we live in this sinful world, Jesus has dealt with humanity's two biggest enemies: death and separation from God when he died on the cross in our place and then rose again.

Death is no longer something to fear for those who trust in Jesus because it is not the end. Though the process of dying will always be hard to experience, for the Christian death is the moment that they go to be with their Lord. Likewise, separation from God is no longer a reality for all those who put their trust in Jesus. He has made it possible for a sinful humanity to be in relationship with a holy God. While our relationship with God was once estranged and broken, through Jesus we're now given the opportunity to be reconciled with God. We can enjoy a good relationship with God again. And one day God will live with his people forever in heaven. True and lasting hope is only found in Jesus because he is the only one who can crush the serpent and reconcile us to God.

7

GRACE

The LORD *God made garments of skin for Adam and his wife and clothed them.* (Genesis 3:21)

When we read of judgment and curses, of sin and death, we might be tempted to think that God is cruel. We might be tempted to see him as an old man who enjoys enforcing unnecessarily harsh rules on people and bursts out in anger when they disobey. We might even be tempted to compare his anger with ours, which is often irrational and out of proportion. But that is not the God we encounter in the Bible.

In the Bible we meet a God who wants to live with his people, a God who wants communion with his creation. Even after the rebellion of Genesis 3, we see God showing grace by acting to give Adam and Eve what they don't deserve. It would have been just for God to have kicked Adam and Eve out of the Garden of Eden and left them to fend for themselves entirely. God had every right to reject his creation because they had rejected him. But, in grace, God clothed Adam and Eve.

In Genesis 3:21, we see that God gives Adam and Eve animal skins, providing them with protection and covering their shame. It is also the first sign of what would later become the sacrificial system, whereby animals were sacrificed as a reminder of the seriousness of our sin and the need for punishment to be carried out. The animals died for Adam and Eve's protection. But these sacrifices and these garments were not sufficient to cover the sins of the whole of humanity. They were pictures, or foreshadows, of the greater sacrifice and the greater sign of grace that would come in the future.

Fast forward in time and God's grace continues to be shown to his people: the nation of Israel. Time and time again they reject God and his laws, and yet God continues to care and provide for them. He continues to call them to repentance, even as they deliberately act defiantly towards the God who saved them from slavery in Egypt, famine and their enemies.

Every breath that we take is a sign of God's grace. We naturally reject our Creator and yet, in his grace, he continues to bless us with life every day. But God doesn't just provide the bare essentials for life. Nor does God stop at animal skins as a solution to our shame.

In the greatest act of divine grace possible, God sent his Son, as God in human flesh, to a sinful world. Not only did Jesus reveal who God is to the world, but he made it possible for our shame and sin to be completely removed from us by becoming the ultimate sacrifice. The skin of an animal is a temporary covering that wears out over time and will eventually fall to pieces. But the righteousness of Jesus – that is, his right standing before God, which has been given to all those who believe in him – will never fail nor fade.

Think of it like a shirt. On the cross, Jesus took our sin-stained shirt on himself and gave us his perfectly clean shirt. Because of Jesus' perfect, right standing before God, all those who believe in him will be covered by his perfect righteousness forever.

Grace is not just an add-on topic in the Bible; it's not an afterthought from a usually mean and distant God. Grace can be seen on every page of the Bible as God lavishes gifts and blessings on his people all the time. The fact that you woke up this morning, are able to read this book and learn more of Jesus and all he has done for you is a wonderful gift of grace. Everyone is alive because God is gracious. Christians know God because he is gracious. Believers are clothed in Christ's righteousness by God's grace. That grace should lead us to praise God for his power, to be in awe of his majesty and to honour him for his goodness and faithfulness to a sinful world. This wonderful news will change your life forever.

8

NOAH

So God said to Noah, 'I am going to put an end to all people, for the earth is filled with violence because of them. I am surely going to destroy both them and the earth. So make yourself an ark of cypress wood; make rooms in it and coat it with pitch inside and out.' (Genesis 6:13–14)

Noah's ark is a familiar story. Children's books show lovely pictures of happy animals sticking their heads out of a wooden boat as they coast along on a calm, still sea. Sure, that picture looks nice and cute when you're a little child. But when we grow up, we realise that Noah's ark isn't a lovely story at all. But it does point forward to something glorious!

In Genesis 3, we see the moment sin entered the world. From then on, as we see in Genesis 4–6, the situation goes from bad to worse as sin increases. Murder happens. Lies lead to family feuds. The whole world is stained by sin. It is not a pretty picture. The world seems beyond repair and beyond any means of salvation.

As we have already seen rebellion against God must be punished. The world is so engulfed in sin that God decides to send a flood. God hits the reset button. But God sees the faithfulness of Noah and saves him and his family. Noah and his family are given instructions to build an ark. Imagine how their neighbours would have felt as they watched this construction. Imagine what the town said about them behind their back. Noah was probably mocked and ridiculed for his obedience to God, but he stands firm. Noah trusts the Lord and acts in obedience. As a result, Noah and his family are saved from the destruction caused by a worldwide flood.

As time passes, the flood waters subside. God puts a rainbow in the sky as a sign that he would never flood the entire world again. That reminder remains today. But, sadly, sin also remains today as well, because it is entrenched in the human heart. Sin isn't only the wrong things that we do or say or think. Sin is like a disease that has penetrated every aspect of our lives. We deserve to have another worldwide flood, but God remains faithful to his promises.

The requirement for a just punishment for our rebellion against God still stands. Yet God, in his abundant love and mercy, has provided a way for that punishment to be taken from us. Salvation from judgment is possible, but this time not through a wooden boat.

Humanity is saved through the death of one person. Salvation is made possible through the completed work of Jesus. In his abundant love and mercy, Jesus became like one of us and stepped into our sin-stained world. The Son of God took on flesh and was nailed to a cross so that we might have the life for which we were created. Noah and his family were saved by their wooden boat, but people are saved through Jesus' death on a wooden cross. Jesus died so that we might live. We are reconciled to God and are given eternal life.

Noah's ark is a reminder of the severity of judgment that awaits all those who do not trust in Jesus. But this story is also a reminder of the great hope of new life that is made possible through Jesus. Noah was saved from the judgment of the flood because of his faith in God, shown in his obedience to build and enter the ark. In the same way that Noah had to be in the ark to be safe from God's judgment, we have to be safe in Jesus. It is only through his death and resurrection that we are saved. Judgment against sin must happen, but Christians, those who are sheltering in Jesus, are saved.

9

BLESSING TO THE WORLD

I will make you into a great nation,
and I will bless you;
I will make your name great,
and you will be a blessing.
I will bless those who bless you,
and whoever curses you I will curse;
and all peoples on earth
will be blessed through you. (Genesis 12:2–3)

'Blessed' is a word that can be used in so many different settings. Social media posts of big houses and fast cars feature the hashtag '#Blessed'. People might describe themselves as blessed if they have a big family or a good job or are content with their lives. The word 'blessed' is often used to describe material things or certain relationships. While this isn't necessarily wrong, the Bible's use of the word 'blessed' is much broader.

In the Old Testament, God reveals himself to one of Noah's descendants called Abram (later known as Abraham) and promises to bless him. He also promises that Abram will have many descendants whom God will make into a nation that will bless the whole world. God certainly does bless Abram – he becomes very rich and the father of a great nation. We also see throughout the Old Testament how Abraham's descendants are to be a blessing to the world. God reveals who he is and his character to them, and gives them the law by which to live. God tells them the correct way to worship him, even giving them the sacrificial system that points to their need for forgiveness in order to be made right with God. The nation of Israel – Abraham's descendants – is to be a light in the world and thus a blessing to the world.

Sadly, Israel doesn't always show the surrounding nations what God is like. They make mistakes, rebelling against God. They worship idols and run after other gods. A lot of the time in the Old Testament you see God's people selfishly focusing on themselves at the neglect of the less fortunate and others around them. (For example, Israel is regularly reminded of their failure to care for and protect the widows, orphans and the poor – see Deuteronomy 10:12–22.) Reading that, maybe you can see similarities with how even Christians today can treat God and others around them.

Does this mean that God fails to follow through on his promise? No! God *does* bless the whole world through the descendants of Abraham, not least through the birth of Jesus, who was born a descendant of Abraham.

The birth of Jesus is the source of blessing for the whole world because it is through him that a right relationship with God is made possible. Romans 4 says that all Christians are descendants of Abraham, because we have received the promises of God through faith and have been given the righteousness of Jesus – but we're in a better place in history than Abraham because we know how the whole story of Jesus unfolds. In addition, the good news about the new life that Jesus offers to those who come to him is being spread all over the world as you read this sentence. At this very moment in time, God is continuing to fulfil his promise to Abraham that through his descendants God will bless the whole world.

The greatest blessing that this world has ever known, and will ever know, is the message that through Jesus people can be made right with God. The broken relationship that has been our reality since the Garden of Eden is not the end of the story. This relationship can be restored.

In Jesus, Christians have received the biggest blessing possible.

10

ABRAHAM AND ISAAC

> *Then God said, 'Take your son, your only son, whom you love – Isaac – and go to the region of Moriah. Sacrifice him there as a burnt offering on a mountain I will show you.'* (Genesis 22:2)

God renames Abram 'Abraham', meaning 'father of many'. Having been promised a descendant, Abraham is looking forward to having a family. But that promise doesn't happen until Abraham is 100 years old (and his wife Sarah is now 90 and has never been able to have children!). Abraham has been waiting for a long time for God to fulfil this promise, but, as we read in Genesis 21, eventually Abraham and Sarah have a son who they name Isaac.

So imagine the shock in Genesis 22 when Abraham is told to take their only son on a journey to offer him as a burnt offering. That seems awful to us: why would a good God ask someone to sacrifice their son? It could make us question God's goodness and love for his people. But if we understand what is really going on here, we see how this story is a signpost that points to Jesus.

Going somewhere that you know will not be pleasant is never a fun experience. No one enjoys going to the doctor's when they know that they're having some invasive tests. The closer we get, each step seems harder than the last. So put yourself in Abraham's shoes for a second. He'd been promised a son, who was finally born when Abraham was 100 years old. He was then told to travel to a mountain and offer his son as a burnt offering. With every step closer to that mountain, the harder his journey must have become. You can imagine him playing through the whole ordeal in his head.

The moment he has dreaded comes. Isaac, understandably confused by the lack of a lamb for the burnt offering, asks, 'where is the lamb for the burnt offering?' (verse 7). Abraham responds, in faith, that the Lord 'will provide' (verse 8).

Crunch time arrives. Isaac is bound on top of a pile of wood and the knife is raised in the air in Abraham's hand. He's ready to offer his son to the Lord. But then an angel speaks and Isaac is spared. Abraham was right: the Lord does provide. Abraham finds a ram that he sacrifices in Isaac's place.

This story is a hard one for us to understand. We gasp – surely asking a father to kill his only son is an impossible task. I would not like to have been in Abraham's position that day. But we come before a God who has been in that position, and who did what Abraham didn't have to – for us.

Genesis 22 isn't just a story of God's grace to this little family, but is a story of the Lord's wonderful provision of a ram. This all points forward to Jesus, who becomes the Lamb of God. Like Isaac, Jesus is God's only Son and deeply loved by his Father. Like Isaac, Jesus carried the wood up towards the place of sacrifice. Like Isaac, Jesus was ready to be offered up. But whereas Abraham did not have to go through with killing his son, God the Father gave Jesus to die for us. As John 3:16 wonderfully puts it "For God so loved the world that he gave his one and only Son, that whoever believes in him shall not perish but have eternal life."

Reading Genesis 22 in isolation might appear mean and cruel. But when read in light of Jesus, the Lamb that the Lord provided, it becomes a wonderful story of provision that should push us towards God, not away from him.

Isaac is a shadow, a signpost to the ultimate Son that the Lord would provide. Jesus is the promised offspring who would end the enmity between God and humanity. Jesus is the promised descendant who would defeat Satan and put an end to the punishment of sin for those who call on his name. Jesus is the promised sacrifice who would be the ultimate blessing to the world because through him people can be made right with God.

11

'I AM'

God said to Moses, 'I AM WHO I AM. This is what you are to say to the Israelites: "I AM has sent me to you."' (Exodus 3:14)

I enjoy reading people's bio sections on Facebook, Twitter and Instagram. It's quite hard to describe yourself in just a sentence or two! We normally start with our birthplace, age and job, then throw in a few hobbies for fun. When asked to identify ourselves, we talk about things that distinguish us from other people.

One of the important ways God describes himself is in Exodus 3. Abraham's family has grown and become a nation, as God promised, but the people are enslaved in Egypt. God reveals himself to an Israelite living in the desert called Moses and gives him a job: to go and free the Israelites, who have been slaves in Egypt for hundreds of years. But Moses is unsure of his ability to carry out this task and makes excuses. When God promises to go with Moses, he asks for God's name so that he can tell the Israelites that God has sent him. God reveals his name, or his identity, as 'I AM'.

I don't think 'I am' is going to be topping a best baby names list any time soon. It sounds a bit odd to us. But there is a lot packed into those three letters. God is revealing that he always was, always is and always will be. God is unchanging. He is the one who promised many wonderful things to Abraham concerning the people of Israel. He is the God of Isaac and Jacob, Abraham's descendants and the forefathers of the Israelites. God is revealing his identity to Moses to give him confidence that God will enable Moses to complete the task at hand. Moses needs reassuring because the task seems impossible.

Fast forward to the New Testament and we see Jesus make some similarly dramatic revelations. Seven times in John's Gospel Jesus describes himself with an 'I am' statement. For example,

Jesus says, 'I am the bread of life' (John 6:35) and 'I am the light of the world' (John 8:12). Jesus uses metaphors in each 'I am' statement to help his hearers understand more about his identity.

Every Jew hearing Jesus' 'I am' statements would have thought back to Exodus 3. But so that there is no doubt in their minds about who Jesus is, he says in John 8:58, 'before Abraham was born, I am!' Jesus is saying, in no uncertain terms, that he is God! That he is the one who has always been, always is and will always be.

Imagine you're back on the Emmaus Road with Cleopas and his friend and heading away from Jerusalem. You're devastated that Jesus has been killed. Hurt that it all seems to be over. Discouraged that maybe he isn't really from God after all. It's in that moment that the disciples need to be shown Jesus' true identity: he is God. Knowing that truth can give us great confidence today too.

Maybe you're still trying to figure out who Jesus is, or maybe you are a Christian but have so many questions about the implications of his identity. The Bible leaves us in no doubt. Jesus is 'I AM'. He has always been, he always is and he promises to always be. There is no greater, no more dependable person than Jesus. Knowing his identity will change your life.

I find it comforting, in an ever-changing world, to know that there is always one constant. Jesus is reliable and trustworthy. Even in the darkest of times, you can always rely on him.

12

THE PASSOVER LAMB

Then Moses summoned all the elders of Israel and said to them, 'Go at once and select the animals for your families and slaughter the Passover lamb. Take a bunch of hyssop, dip it into the blood in the basin and put some of the blood on the top and on both sides of the doorframe. None of you shall go out of the door of your house until morning.' (Exodus 12:21–22)

If someone were to describe you as a lamb, you probably wouldn't be happy. Today, it's a pet name used for cute kids. A lamb is typically seen as a defenceless, innocent, unassuming, cuddly little thing. But, surprisingly, it's a lamb that brings about protection for the nation of Israel and ultimately salvation.

Moses eventually goes to Egypt, as the Lord instructed him, and speaks to Pharaoh about allowing the Israelites to leave. Pride and hardness of heart kick in and Pharaoh refuses to let the people go. The Lord sends plagues upon the Egyptians for their treatment of the Lord's people and Pharaoh's refusal to let the Israelites go. Each plague takes its toll. Each plague is horrible in its own way and would be enough to make most people listen to God. But not Pharaoh.

The final plague is the worst: all the firstborn boys will die. But the Lord tells his people to prepare a lamb and spread its blood over the doorposts of their home to protect their firstborn. You can imagine the conversations going on in the Israelite homes that night. You can almost feel the parents' dread as they spread the blood and hug their firstborn, wondering if that blood will be enough. You can sense the fear as people put their hope in the blood of an innocent lamb. Midnight comes and the Lord takes the lives of all the firstborn sons and animals in the land of Egypt, except those who have covered their doors with lamb's blood. Ultimately, though, it is not the lamb that saves them but their obedience to God. They act as he tells them to do. Their confidence is not in a lamb, but in the Lord and his faithfulness.

Fast forward to the early days of Jesus' life on earth. The people, who are on the lookout for the Messiah, are seeing the things of God happening and have heard Jesus' cousin John the Baptist calling people to repent. They are talking about John wondering who he might be (John 1:19–28). John is asked if he is the Messiah, the one they have been expecting God to send to save his people. No, John says, he isn't the Messiah. He's asked if he is Elijah or a prophet. No, John says, he isn't those either.

Maybe they expect their Messiah to be a knight in shining armour – someone to kick out the Romans and make Israel independent and strong. Maybe they are expecting a Messiah who is as voracious as a lion, someone who would take on any challenge and be a symbol of strength and bravery. But instead, John the Baptist points them to the Lamb.

In John 1:29, John sees Jesus and says, 'Look, the Lamb of God, who takes away the sin of the world!' This is another time when the people of God will have to put their trust in the blood of a lamb. But it is different. This Lamb is not one of many being killed to protect people; his blood is a once-for-all sacrifice. The blood of Jesus, the Lamb of God, is shed for the Lord's people so that their sins are fully taken away. Completely blotted out. Obliterated. All of those who have put their trust in Jesus have been freed from the punishment that they are due for their sins.

Every Passover, the Jews remembered how God delivered them from Egypt. Every time Christians celebrate communion together we too remember a time when we were saved from our slavery to sin. By eating bread and drinking wine, Christians remember how Jesus' body was broken and his blood poured out for us.

The Lamb lived a perfect life and yet, according to God's perfect will, was crucified. This Lamb is the Lamb of God – the Lord's wonderful provision and the greatest gift to humanity.

13

CROSSING THE RED SEA

But the Israelites went through the sea on dry ground, with a wall of water on their right and on their left. That day the LORD saved Israel from the hands of the Egyptians, and Israel saw the Egyptians lying dead on the shore. And when the Israelites saw the mighty hand of the LORD displayed against the Egyptians, the people feared the LORD and put their trust in him and in Moses his servant. (Exodus 14:29–31)

I find it interesting to see how quick we are to sanitise some Bible stories. The parting of the Red Sea, for example, is the topic of many memes and funny comic strips, ranging from

Moses as a baby parting the bath water and a fish being late for work because the sea became dry land. The crossing of the Red Sea comes at the moment that Israel, just released from slavery, is on the run. Their oppressors are hot on their heels, trying to force them back into slavery, but God does a miracle. As the Israelites face the sea, with the Egyptians behind them, God parts the water, allowing the Israelites to escape in safety and on dry land.

But reading about the parting of the Red Sea is a little bit like being in a house of mirrors attraction. As you look in the mirror, you see your reflection. When you then tilt to the side a little, you see your reflection is duplicated multiple times. The crossing of the Red Sea is not just about the miraculous escape of the Israelites. Viewed from a different perspective, it teaches us about the might and power of God.

In my experience, the sea doesn't just part and become dry land. It is impossible for a human to recreate this miracle. But the God who spoke the world into being, the God who holds the winds and the seas in their place, can make it happen. The parting of the Red Sea shows Israel that their God is fighting for them, providing safety and deliverance from their enemies. I'm sure the Israelites were scared as they looked towards the water and looked back at the Egyptian chariots coming to attack them all. I can imagine that some of them were asking themselves, 'Does God really care if we die here?' But in a display of his might and power, God does the impossible and parts the sea for his people.

Now jump forward in time and picture yourself with the disciples on a boat in the middle of a raging storm. Seasoned fishermen are afraid for their lives while Jesus sleeps in the back. So the disciples ask, 'Teacher, don't you care if we drown?' (Mark 4:38). In an act of might and power, Jesus – God in the flesh – stands up and commands the winds and the sea to be still, and they obey him. Immediately, peace and tranquillity comes over the winds and the waves, and all is still. The whole point is that Jesus, being God, has power over nature.

God makes the impossible possible. By acts of mighty power, he commands the forces of nature to both teach and protect his people. The same is true both in the Old Testament, with Israel's crossing of the Red Sea, and in the New Testament, when Jesus calms the storm. Jesus wasn't resting in the boat because he didn't care for the lives of the disciples. Jesus was resting because he knew that he could make the wind and the waves obey him, because he is God.

14

THE LAW

Then Moses went up to God, and the LORD called to him from the mountain and said, 'This is what you are to say to the descendants of Jacob and what you are to tell the people of Israel: "You yourselves have seen what I did to Egypt, and how I carried you on eagles' wings and brought you to myself. Now if you obey me fully and keep my covenant, then out of all nations you will be my treasured possession. Although the whole earth is mine, you will be for me a kingdom of priests and a holy nation." These are the words you are to speak to the Israelites.' (Exodus 19:3–6)

Some rules are easier to follow than others. Maybe you're like me and when you see a 'stay off the grass' sign, you can't help but want to gently press your foot on the lush green grass. But not all rules are bad. We would be wise to listen to many of them. Some rules protect human life (such as not killing or harming others). Other rules are intended for our own safety and well-being (for example, warning us not to touch something hot or go to dangerous places).

After crossing the Red Sea, the nation of Israel camp in the desert on their way to the land God has promised them. It is here that God gives them his laws by which they are to live. These touch on every area of life: marriage, ceremonial worship (how they are to worship the Lord), the sacrificial system (how they need to be forgiven by God), justice and the conduct of the whole nation. These laws are given to them for a number of reasons.

Firstly, the law shows them their sinfulness (Romans 3:20). These laws were impossible to fully uphold because, as we have already seen, humanity is stained by sin. So the law is to remind the Israelites that humanity is sinful and in need of forgiveness. They are also reminded of this truth by the sacrificial system. The act of sacrificing animals as substitutes for the sins of people is a physical reminder that the ultimate punishment for sin is death.

Secondly, the law shows how an unholy people need to live in order for a holy God to dwell with them. God's holiness means that he is perfect, spotless and without fault. Perfection and sin do not, and cannot, mix. So something needs to change to make this relationship between a perfect God and an imperfect people possible. What needs to happen is a change of the human heart. Rather than being sinful and full of pride, people need to humble themselves before God and obey him with all their lives.

Thirdly, the law is given so that the Israelites will be set apart from the other nations and live distinct lives. They are to draw attention to the fact that the God they serve is different from everyone else's gods.

The Old Testament law highlights the important truth that humanity cannot be right with God on our own merit. We can try, as is the case for many people, to do and say the right things, but we need to be changed and transformed from the inside out. We need to be made perfect and be reconciled to God if we are to enjoy a relationship with him.

Jesus, being God in the flesh, was able to fulfil the law and live in absolute obedience to it. Jesus, being born of a virgin, was conceived in Mary's womb by the Holy Spirit (Luke 1:35). He didn't inherit sin. Being perfect, he deserved no punishment. However, he willingly took our sin and unholiness upon himself, giving us his righteousness, his right standing with God. Jesus makes it possible for a sinful humanity to be made right with God.

Jesus also grants new life to all those who follow him. Followers of Jesus have been given a new heart. A Christian is a transformed and new creation, a new person who wants to live and serve Jesus.

15

THE TRUE PROPHET

> *I will raise up for them a prophet like you from among their fellow Israelites, and I will put my words in his mouth. He will tell them everything I command him.* (Deuteronomy 18:18)

Everywhere you look, there are voices influencing you, some quietly and some loudly, some for good and some for bad. It could be the television adverts telling you that you need the newest gadgets. It could be the social media adverts promoting a certain body image that everyone 'needs'. We're surrounded by countless voices, all trying to influence us to live and act a certain way.

This is not a new phenomenon. Even thousands of years ago, when God's people had left Egypt and were on their way across the desert to Canaan, to the Promised Land God had given them to live in, there were different voices trying to influence their thinking. In the book of Deuteronomy, the Israelites are warned about the people who possess the land they're entering. Those inhabitants listen to people who say they consult spirits and practise sorcery. God is warning the Israelites that they are to be different. When they arrive in the Promised Land, they are not supposed to be influenced by the same bad and unhelpful voices.

God has to tell them this because it's natural for people to want to fit in. We want to have a group of friends, and will happily dress or speak a certain way so that we're not too different. But that's not what God wants for his people.

Instead, God promises that he will send them a prophet to instruct them. In the Old Testament, a prophet is a bit like a spokesperson – they bring a message on God's behalf for God's people. And as it's easy for someone to claim to be a prophet, God tells them how they should recognise the one he's going to send.

Firstly, this prophet will be a fellow Israelite. He would be one of them, a person from their own country. The prophet would be someone who knew their laws, their customs, their culture and their language.

Secondly, the prophet will speak what God wants him to say, rather than just saying what he feels would be appropriate or easy in the moment.

Thirdly, the Israelites will know which prophet is good and trustworthy to listen to because what he says will happen will come true. Throughout the Old Testament, God raises up different prophets and sends them to the Israelites with his message. That message differs depending on the situation, but what God says will happen always comes to pass. Every prophecy has been fulfilled except those which point forward to the last day when the Lord Jesus returns.

But God's promise to send the prophet definitely happened. 'Smaller' prophets come along the way, dotted throughout Israel's history. But the ultimate prophet that Deuteronomy 18 speaks about came in the person of Jesus Christ.

As God promised, Jesus was an Israelite, part of God's people. Jesus was born in Bethlehem, a small town in Israel. While his birth might have seemed insignificant at the time, he would change the world. As time went on, this baby grew up and began to teach the people of Israel about God. He did miracles and spoke with an authority that they'd never seen before.

As God promised, Jesus spoke what God wanted him to say – as he explains in John 12:49.

Finally, as God promised, what Jesus said would happen came true. Multiple times throughout his ministry, Jesus stated that he would be killed but then be raised to life again. The disciples didn't believe him. To be fair, neither would we because people don't die and then come back to life. But Jesus isn't just a normal man. Jesus is God in the flesh, doing what we cannot. Everything he does points to God. Everything he does helps those around him to learn more about God and his kingdom. Jesus is *the* Prophet because, as he explains:

> *I have come down from heaven not to do my will but to do the will of him who sent me. And this is the will of him who sent me, that I shall lose none of all those he has given me, but raise them up at the last day. For my Father's will is that everyone who looks to the Son and believes*

in him shall have eternal life, and I will raise them up at the last day (John 6:38–40).

Jesus came as God's prophet to call people to himself, but he was also the sacrifice who was crucified to make that relationship possible.

If there's ever a voice that we should all listen to, surely it's the voice of the one who created us, giving us life and purpose. The best voice we can listen to is the voice of God's prophet Jesus, who calls us to join him.

16

THE TRUE KING

In those days and at that time
I will make a righteous Branch sprout
from David's line;
he will do what is just and
right in the land.
In those days Judah will be saved
and Jerusalem will live in safety.
This is the name by which it will be called:
The LORD Our Righteous Saviour.
(Jeremiah 33:15–16)

We all look for people to follow. We want to have examples that we can model. For a child, their natural example is their parents, so children will often adopt the mannerisms and habits of their parents. Most of these will be good, but the occasional bad one slips through the net. Adults want examples too, maybe looking up to our bosses, famous people or possibly even some world leaders. However, it's not always good to imitate the lives of leaders.

In the Old Testament, Israel were given kings and leaders to rule over them. Originally, God was their ruler and their King. But desiring to be like those around them, the Israelites wanted a human king. The Lord graciously granted them their wish, but he also warned them of the dangers of having a sinful human being rule over them. However, they did not listen.

The Lord raised up kings and leaders from the Israelites and gave them laws that they should follow. These laws were designed to keep the leaders and kings on the right path, helping them live in a way that glorified God and benefitted his people. But that wasn't always the case. Some kings were bad and did evil things, living contrary to God's law and his wishes for his people. While other kings, largely speaking, led well, they were still sinners. King David, for example, is known as a man after God's own heart, and yet he used his position of power to commit adultery and then murder the husband.

King Solomon was a wise and wealthy ruler, and yet his heart was torn and distracted from God and his law because of his multitude of wives.

Each of these Old Testament kings was supposed to be a ruler who was led by the Lord to govern his people well. The Lord had blessed the people with a land, wonderful promises and laws to follow. But the kings sinned because they were sinful human beings, just like us. We can try our hardest to be 'good people', but ultimately we will always fail because we don't have the capability to resist sin.

God's people needed a perfect leader who was unaffected by sin and worthy to rule them. The king promised in Jeremiah 33:15–16 would be God's rightful King who would do good and save God's people. In the Old Testament, we get glimpses of this ultimate King – one who will rule in all wisdom and power. The King who will govern with might and with justice. The King whose kingdom will never fade or perish, but will continue for all of time. This King cannot be a human being. This King must be perfect. Therefore, he must be God.

During his earthly ministry, Jesus speaks about the kingdom of God. He says his kingdom 'is not of this world' (John 18:36). In Jesus, we see God's King calling God's people into God's kingdom. This was ultimately made possible through Jesus' death on the cross. That's why, in Revelation 17:14, Jesus, the 'King of kings', is described as the conquering Lamb, who will ultimately 'triumph over' all his enemies surrounded by his 'chosen and faithful followers'.

Revelation 19:13 also draws on the imagery of Jesus' sacrifice: 'He is dressed in a robe dipped in blood, and his name is the Word of God.' Then verse 16 is unambiguous – on Jesus' robe is written his name: 'KING OF KINGS AND LORD OF LORDS.'

As we seek someone to follow, a leader to give allegiance to, we should look to Jesus. He alone is the true and ultimate King of God. He is the only King that is worthy of all of our praise and he is the only King who died and rose again so that his people can have life, and life to the full.

17

THE TRUE SERVANT

Here is my servant, whom I uphold,
my chosen one in whom I delight;
I will put my Spirit on him,
and he will bring justice to the nations.
(Isaiah 42:1)

I wonder what springs to mind when you think of a servant. Maybe you think of a character like Dobby from the Harry Potter series, a creature who is locked into a life of servitude to his master. Or perhaps you think of a personal assistant, who is employed to do the day-to-day tasks of someone else. Jesus shows us a radically different type of servanthood to either of these popular images.

In the Old Testament, we're told about the coming Servant of the Lord. The book of Isaiah has four Servant Songs. Each of these songs gives us an insight into who Jesus is and what he did. If you take a step back from them, you get a grand view of Jesus, the true and perfect Servant of the Lord.

ISAIAH 42:1–9

The Servant of the Lord is described as the one who brings true justice. One who protects and cares for the poor and marginalised, and who sets the captive free. Jesus regularly surrounded himself with sinners, broken people in need of a Saviour. The religious elite hated him for it, even though if they obeyed God's law, they would also have made sure that justice was upheld.

ISAIAH 49:1–7

Isaiah predicts that the Servant of the Lord will call people to God. He will be a light to the nations and call the Lord's people back to living faithful and obedient lives. But Isaiah acknowledges too that this Servant will be despised by the nations. While Jesus called people into God's kingdom, he was criticised by the religious leaders of his day and ultimately was crucified by the Romans. Then after his resurrection, the message of Jesus' life and light spread to many nations, and continues to do so today.

ISAIAH 50:4–9

Isaiah tell us that the Servant of the Lord will not be rebellious, never turning away from the Lord's commands. Jesus is the true Servant because he obeyed God's law perfectly. He lived the perfect life of obedience that the Israelites never could, and that we never can, because he is God. Jesus was the perfect servant who suffered death, even though he was innocent, because he knew that was the Lord's will to bring about salvation for his people. Even now, Jesus continues to serve us as, seated at the right hand of God, he intercedes on our behalf, praying to God for us (Romans 8:34).

ISAIAH 52:13 – 53:12

This final Servant song brings together all the themes of the previous three. The Servant of the Lord is crowned victorious through suffering. The Lord's Servant will be beaten and wounded, not for his own sins, but for the sins of his people. This song is a vivid picture of what we see at Jesus' trial and crucifixion. But the story of the Lord's Servant does not end in misery and tragedy:

> *After he has suffered,*
> *he will see the light of life and be satisfied;*
> *by his knowledge my righteous servant*
> *will justify many,*
> *and he will bear their iniquities.*
> *Therefore I will give him a portion*
> *among the great,*
> *and he will divide the spoils with the strong,*
> *because he poured out his life unto death,*
> *and was numbered with the transgressors.*
> *For he bore the sin of many,*
> *and made intercession for the transgressors*
> *(Isaiah 53:11–12).*

Jesus rose from the dead victorious and he reigns at the right hand of God in all power and splendour.

Looking at these four descriptions of Jesus gives us a fuller picture of Jesus' identity and actions. Jesus is both King and Servant, the mighty and the lowly. Jesus is the true and perfect Servant of the Lord.

18

THE ULTIMATE HIGH PRIEST

For we do not have a high priest who is unable to feel sympathy for our weaknesses, but we have one who has been tempted in every way, just as we are – yet he did not sin. Let us then approach God's throne of grace with confidence, so that we may receive mercy and find grace to help us in our time of need.
(Hebrews 4:15–16)

The book of Leviticus is full of rules and laws, given by God to the people of Israel for their day-to-day life, including their worship. Certain people were given roles and jobs to do in order to ensure that the people of God worshipped God how he said they should.

Priests were chosen from the Israelite tribe of Levi. These priests were tasked with the daily religious running of the tabernacle, a portable sanctuary where people worshipped God before they were fully settled in the Promised Land. Once King Solomon built a permanent temple, that too was overseen by the Levites. They were responsible for everything related to the worship of God. These priests were different from today's local church leaders. These Levite priests had a special role in performing sacrifices on behalf of the people.

But there was an even greater role: that of the high priest. He was basically the boss of the temple, overseeing all the sacrifices and in charge of keeping everything functioning as it should. The high priest's most important job was going into the holy of holies once a year. This was a special part of the temple where God's presence dwelt and was separated by a big curtain. The curtain represented the barrier that needed to be in place between a holy God and an unholy people.

The high priest would enter the holy of holies to burn incense and sprinkle blood as a sign of the need for forgiveness – both for his own sins and for the sins of God's people. But do you see the problem? It had to happen every year! The high priest couldn't ensure the permanent forgiveness of sins.

While the book of Leviticus spends a lot of time detailing the sacrifices needed and the role of the priesthood, the book of Hebrews in the New Testament tells us about the fulfilment of both. Hebrews 10:4 says that the blood of animals could not 'take away sins'. Instead, a greater sacrifice was needed – a sacrifice so perfect and so great that it would not have to be repeated. That sacrifice was Jesus.

But Jesus is not only the sacrifice, he is also the true High Priest, as Hebrews 4:14 – 5:10 describes. In the Old Testament, the high priest was selected from the people of Israel and made their representative before God. The role was given to him, not chosen by him. Jesus also was given his role of High Priest by God the Father. And as our High Priest, he represents his people before the Father in heaven. Jesus knows our weakness because he was tested like we are – and yet he didn't sin. Now seated at the right hand of God the Father, he is praying and interceding for his people. The Old Testament high priest was a foreshadow of the perfect and true High Priest, Jesus.

Jesus, being both fully God and fully man, is able to fulfil the role of the true High Priest because he has unhindered access to the Father. Whereas, in the Old Testament, the high priest could only enter into the holy of holies once a year, Jesus has constant access to the throne room of God and therefore is the perfect forever priest.

19

THE KINSMAN REDEEMER

> *If one of your fellow Israelites becomes poor and sells some of their property, their nearest relative is to come and redeem what they have sold. If, however, there is no one to redeem it for them but later on they prosper and acquire sufficient means to redeem it themselves … they can then go back to their own property.*
> (Leviticus 25:25–27)

There are some things in the Bible that can seem strange to a 21st-century mind. One such thing is the kinsman redeemer, a relative who would assume the responsibility of a deceased family member in order to continue the deceased's family line and their legacy. While to the modern mind it sounds odd for a family member to redeem what a relative had lost, the principle comes from Leviticus 25:25: 'If one of your fellow Israelites becomes poor and sells some of their property, their nearest relative is to come and redeem what they have sold.' This principle applied to anything that was lost, whether that be property, the freedom of someone who had sold themselves into slavery to pay a debt, or even a person's name and their family.

The most well-known Old Testament example is in the book of Ruth. Ruth, originally from Moab, married an Israelite man. After some time, Ruth's husband died, and so did both her father-in-law and her brother-in-law. Ruth went back to Bethlehem with her mother-in-law, Naomi. They returned there in hope of food and provision.

Boaz, a landowner, saw Ruth gleaning in the fields and made enquiries about her. Boaz was a relative of Ruth's dead husband and so took on the role of a kinsman redeemer. This meant that he would marry Ruth and take responsibility for her deceased husband's property, ensuring this got passed down to their firstborn son rather than to any of Boaz's other children.

For a person to qualify as a kinsman redeemer, a few things needed to be true:

You needed to be related to the person.

Leviticus 25:25 says that it must be their nearest relative.

You needed to want to be the kinsman redeemer.

In Ruth's case, there was a closer relative than Boaz (Ruth 4:1–6), but he was not willing to be the kinsman redeemer.

You needed the means to be the kinsman redeemer.

You couldn't just say you wanted to do so; you actually needed the means to be able to pay the debt, or settle whatever needed to be settled, as per the law in Leviticus 25:25–28.

You needed to redeem all or nothing.

In Ruth 4, Boaz spoke to the closer relative and told him everything that he would have to redeem. The closer relative was unwilling lest his own estate be endangered. Being a kinsman redeemer was an all-or-nothing job.

So, how does this kinsman redeemer point us to Jesus? Today, our redemption isn't bound up in terms of land, possession or names, but we all need redeeming from the sin that plagues the entire world. This is how Jesus is our Kinsman Redeemer. Let's apply those same principles:

Jesus became one of us.

John 1:14 says that Jesus became human and dwelt among us. He was tempted and tested like we are and yet he did not sin. Jesus humbled himself and stepped into our world. He became one of us.

Jesus wanted to redeem us.

Philippians 2:5–11 is a wonderful passage about Jesus and what he did by becoming one of us. It makes it very clear that Jesus humbled himself and became one of us so that he could go to the cross, be raised to life and restore us to God the Father. Jesus willingly did that.

Jesus had the means.

It's pointless to be willing to redeem someone, but not have the means to do so. Each of us has inherited the nature of sin through the disobedience of the first man, Adam. This is called original sin. Since Genesis 3, the entire human race has been plagued with sin; we cannot escape it. But just as we have all been made sinners through the disobedience of one man, we can be made righteous through the perfect obedience of one man, Jesus (Romans 5:12–19). Only Jesus, being fully God, had the means to be able to redeem his people.

Jesus paid it all.

There are plenty of places in the New Testament where we could go to see the complete redemption that Jesus made possible through his life, death, resurrection and ascension. However, Titus 2:11–14 sums it up wonderfully. Jesus died 'to redeem us from all wickedness and to purify for himself a people that are his very own' (verse 14).

Jesus is the perfect Redeemer who continues to save people today, paying their debt and giving them his righteousness.

PART 2:

THE SIGNPOSTS POINT HERE

20

MUCH MORE THAN A BABY

For to us a child is born,
to us a son is given,
and the government will be on
his shoulders.
And he will be called
Wonderful Counsellor, Mighty God,
Everlasting Father, Prince of Peace.
(Isaiah 9:6)

If you've followed along thus far, or even if you've just glanced over the last few chapters or chapter headings, you'll have realised that Jesus is much more than just a man or a moral teacher. Maybe, like many people in the world today, you have the traditional picture of the nativity story in mind at Christmas time. Perhaps you think about Jesus as just another cute baby.

But Jesus is much more than a baby in a manger. Seven hundred years before Jesus was even born, the book of Isaiah gives us four descriptions of who he is and just how powerful he would be. These descriptions were promises given by God in a time of great darkness. This promised future child would be the light and hope that they longed for and needed.

Jesus is described as:

1. WONDERFUL COUNSELLOR

Counsellors today use a variety of methods to help people be mentally and emotionally healthy. But often the focus is that the 'fix' is within the person. Jesus is not a counsellor who comes alongside us and tells us to try harder or to be better. He is a counsellor who draws alongside the weak and the broken-hearted, steps into our pain and guides us on the right path. Jesus knows pain and suffering, and he draws near to us in ours to bring comfort.

2. MIGHTY GOD

When we look at the Jesus clearly presented in the Bible, we see the very image of the invisible God. That's what Colossians 1:15–20 is all about. It says that God has shown us what he is like in Jesus, and also that Jesus is the leader of the church and the one who holds together everything in creation. Jesus is the one through whom and for whom all things were created. We see this in Mark's Gospel too. In Mark 4:35 – 5:43, Jesus has power over nature, evil, sickness and even death; he calms the storm, casts out a demon, heals a sick woman and raises a little girl to life. Jesus is much more than a baby in a manger; he is the Mighty God.

3. EVERLASTING FATHER

It's strange to think of Jesus as the everlasting Father, because we normally use that terminology for God the Father. However, this description conveys two things about Jesus.

The first is that he is everlasting. Jesus' life did not begin some two thousand years ago in ancient Israel. When John introduces Jesus, he takes us right back to the beginning: 'In the beginning was the Word, and the Word was with God, and the Word was God. He was with God in the beginning ... The Word became flesh and made his dwelling among us' (John 1:1 and 14). Jesus does not have a beginning or an end, but is everlasting.

The second thing this description teaches us is that Jesus is like a father. Good fathers love their children. As we look at the life of Jesus, there can be no doubt in our minds that he loved people. He sat with those on the fringes of society. He gravitated towards those deemed unfit or broken. He had compassion on people and healed the sick. Jesus is described as 'Everlasting Father' because he has always been and will always be, and he loves his children with a love that goes beyond our wildest imaginations.

4. PRINCE OF PEACE

As the nation of Israel were awaiting an incoming army, which is the context of this passage from Isaiah 9, they would have been longing for peace. The peace that Jesus offers, though, is far greater than peace from war and peace within one nation. The peace that Jesus offers is twofold.

Firstly, it means peace with God. Jesus, being the perfect sacrifice, has taken the punishment we deserve and enabled us to be made right with God. This means a restored relationship with God. It means that we begin to live the life that we were created to live.

Secondly, it means eternal and final peace in the future. This is the eternal peace that is only possible through Jesus. It refers to the glorious new heavens and new earth where God and people will dwell together in perfect harmony. No more pain, no more suffering and no more death. And the reign of this Prince of Peace knows no end.

All of these descriptions point to the child who would be born of a virgin 700 years later and who would make relationship with God possible. Thank the Lord that Jesus is so much more than just a baby in a manger.

21

GOD WITH US

Therefore the Lord himself will give you a sign: the virgin will conceive and give birth to a son, and will call him Immanuel. (Isaiah 7:14)

Names have an important role to play in some cultures today. For example, Arabic friends are quick to tell you the meaning of their name and why it was given to them. The meanings of names is something that is largely lost in our 21st-century, Western culture. For example, my name means 'defending men' or 'the defender of men'. I highly doubt that my parents looked at me as a newborn and thought that this would be the characterising feature of my life. Looking at me today, I wouldn't say it characterises my life now either.

However, historically, names and their meaning were significant. The same is true as we look at Jesus, both following his birth and also before. In Isaiah 7:14, above, Jesus is given the name Immanuel, meaning 'God with us'.

In the Old Testament, God's presence among his people is a prominent theme. The name 'God with us' reminds God's people about his promises to save, bless and protect them. It also conveys intimacy and proximity. This wasn't possible under the law, which highlighted the sinfulness of man and the perfect holiness of God. The curtain placed in the tabernacle and then the temple signified the distance that was necessary between God and his people. But Isaiah is looking forward to a future day when God's presence with his people will be different. A day when God's presence will be even more intimate than they could have imagined.

Zoom forward 700 years to the birth of Jesus. In Matthew's account, an angel appears to Joseph in a dream and tells him to marry Mary, although she is pregnant, because she has conceived through the Holy Spirit. The angel also instructs Joseph to call the baby Jesus, which means 'the Lord saves'. Then Matthew 1:22–23 explains that the birth of Jesus is a fulfilment of the promise in Isaiah 7 and that Jesus is God with us.

The incarnation, the moment that God the Son took on flesh and came among us in the person of Jesus, is a miracle that we should never fail to wonder at. The fact that Jesus willingly took on flesh and stepped into our world, knowing that he would suffer and be rejected, is a sign of his great love for his people. It was through his suffering that the promise of salvation in 'God with us' became a reality.

The prophet Isaiah told of the wonderful day when God would take on flesh and dwell with his people, and this promise is fulfilled in the birth of Jesus. But Jesus is not dwelling on earth anymore. After rising from the dead, he ascended to heaven, where he sits at the right hand of the Father. In his absence from his people, Jesus has sent the Holy Spirit to be with us. We wait with eager anticipation for the glorious future day when the Lord's presence with his people will be permanent in the new creation:

> *Then I saw 'a new heaven and a new earth,' for the first heaven and the first earth had passed away, and there was no longer any sea.*

I saw the Holy City, the new Jerusalem, coming down out of heaven from God, prepared as a bride beautifully dressed for her husband. And I heard a loud voice from the throne saying, 'Look! God's dwelling-place is now among the people, and he will dwell with them. They will be his people, and God himself will be with them and be their God. "He will wipe every tear from their eyes. There will be no more death" or mourning or crying or pain, for the old order of things has passed away' (Revelation 21:1-4).

22

JESUS BECAME ONE OF US

... what is mankind that you are
mindful of them,
human beings that you care for them?
You have made them a little lower
than the angels
and crowned them with glory and
honour. (Psalm 8:4–5)

We've already seen so many moments in the Old Testament that point forward to Jesus, finding their true fulfilment in him. But Psalm 8 plays a slightly different role. It tells the reader to look back and to look forward.

You could say that Psalm 8 is a little bit like an engagement ring. A woman's engagement ring points back to the date when she agreed to marry her fiancé and is a reminder of the commitment they made. But the ring also points forward to the future day when she will receive a wedding ring and their married life together will begin. Let me explain how Psalm 8 is similar.

In Psalm 8, the writer looks at the world and is amazed at God's wonderful creation. Then, in contrast, the psalmist asks, 'what is mankind that you are mindful of them, human beings that you care for them?' Though people are small in comparison to the greatness of God's created order, God still saw fit to crown humankind with glory and honour and to give them authority over the world. This should draw our attention back to the Garden of Eden, where Adam and Eve were told to govern the world. They were given a central place, greater than the animals and yet 'lower than the angels'.

But since the Fall in Genesis 3, when sin entered the world, humanity's natural focus has not been on God, but on the world around us. In our rebellion, we have turned our back on God, instead seeking our own desires and priorities.

The glory, honour and dominion given in the garden has been tainted and twisted.

However, in addition to looking back at creation, Psalm 8 also encourages us to look forward. We see this more clearly in Hebrews 2, where the author quotes Psalm 8:4–6 to highlight Jesus' humanity. Whereas Hebrews 1 focuses on Jesus' divinity and his superiority over the angels, Hebrews 2 focuses on his role as the perfect human: 'But we do see Jesus, who was made lower than the angels for a little while, now crowned with glory and honour because he suffered death, so that by the grace of God he might taste death for everyone' (verse 9).

Since Genesis 3, it has been impossible for humankind to fully obey the Lord's commands and to fulfil the role he created for us. Jesus became one of us, humbling himself, to do what we never could. He was put lower than the angels, for a time, but was then crowned with glory and honour after his resurrection and ascension.

Humanity once had that position of privilege and honour when we were in a right relationship with God. However, that honour was lost as Adam and Eve rejected him, preferring the darkness over the light. But by God's wonderful grace and love, the Lord sent his Son to restore people's relationship with God and to redeem humanity from the sin that entangles our hearts. Jesus has restored us to the place of glory and honour that we were given at the beginning of the world. Wonderfully 'both the one who makes people holy [Jesus] and those who are made holy [his people] are of the same family. So Jesus is not ashamed to call them brothers and sisters' (Hebrews 2:11).

23

TEACHING IN PARABLES

My people, hear my teaching;
listen to the words of my mouth.
I will open my mouth with a parable;
I will utter hidden things, things from of old. (Psalm 78:1–2)

We all love a good story. We like to hear stories of experiences and examples of truth lived out in someone's life. Jesus spoke in parables, earthy stories with a heavenly meaning. His parables resonated with people and continue to be told today. They were, and still are, a great verbal tool because they drew in people. However, they are often misunderstood.

Jesus used parables to communicate the things of God to people, knowing some would understand and some would not. Those who wanted to know more would ask questions and wrestle with their meaning, but those who didn't would simply see them as interesting stories and nothing more. In the same way, many people today see Jesus' parables as mere moralistic stories to help us live well and be nice people. But such an interpretation of Jesus' words is missing the point.

Psalm 78:1–2 tells us that Jesus would speak in parables. Then, in Matthew 13:1–23, Jesus explains why he taught in parables, referencing both Psalm 78 and Isaiah 6. Jesus was revealing things of God to people, speaking to them of heavenly things that they could not fully understand at that time. But there were those who came to a partial understanding of what Jesus was talking about and followed him. Through Jesus' parables, those who were open to the truth of God learned more truth, but those who were not open to God's truth were hardened to it.

Parables have an element of mystery to them that had not yet been disclosed when

Jesus was teaching. But that mystery was revealed after his death and resurrection as Paul says in Ephesians 3:6: 'This mystery is that through the gospel the Gentiles [non-Jews] are heirs together with Israel, members together of one body, and sharers together in the promise in Christ Jesus.'

The mystery of the gospel has been revealed. Therefore, if you're reading this, or if you hear about Jesus, the mystery of God's goodness to the world has been revealed to you. How you respond really matters. Will you trust in him or not?

Christians need to pray that people's ears would be opened to hear the truth of Jesus. We need to pray that people's eyes would be opened to see who Jesus really is. And we need to tell people the truth of God, but then leave the outcome up to him. God knows who his people are.

Many people in Jesus' day didn't want to hear the truth about God and so they did not hear the meaning of his parables. Every listener was given the opportunity to hear the truth, but many didn't. Likewise, today, our role is to spread the news of Jesus, but not everyone will hear the truth. Some will believe Jesus; others will reject him.

24

SOME LISTEN, OTHERS DON'T

Go and tell this people:
'Be ever hearing, but never understanding;
be ever seeing, but never
perceiving.' (Isaiah 6:9)

Imagine you've been given a job, to take a message to a specific group of people, but they won't listen. That was Isaiah's job. He was to go to the people of Israel and call them to return to the Lord. But God told Isaiah that they would not listen to him (Isaiah 6:9–10).

Was God just wasting Isaiah's time? No, God was giving Israel another chance to respond in repentance and return to him. By refusing to listen, by rejecting God's message through Isaiah, the people had sealed their future under the wrath of God. Isaiah's message was freely proclaimed to all who would hear, but he could not determine who would respond and repent.

Similarly, people's hearts had become calloused in Jesus' time too. Jesus knew the world that he was stepping into. Jesus knew that he would not be welcome on earth and that he was going to a people who would ultimately shout for his crucifixion. John 1 explains it in terms of light. Jesus is the light that came into this world and yet the world did not know him. Jesus was sent to his own people and yet they did not receive him (verses 11–12).

Did God waste Jesus' time? No! Jesus came and lived the perfect life, fulfilling all that was commanded under the Old Testament law. He was the perfect Israelite. God made it clear in the Old Testament that he would send a Messiah, saying what Jesus would do and be for God's people. However, people still chose to reject the message of the kingdom of God that Jesus gave and instead chose darkness.

The people that Jesus was sent to save did not listen or care for him, but crucified him.

Their response was to shut their ears and kill their God-sent King. But what they did with evil intent was God's plan to bring about salvation. Even though not everyone listened to Jesus and his message, he gave his life to pay the price for the sins of the world.

Some people would only realise who Jesus was after seeing him crucified, like the Roman centurion who then confessed about Jesus, 'Surely this man was the Son of God!' (Mark 15:39). Others, while Jesus lived among them, would never see Jesus for who he really was and trust in him. The same is true today.

As Christians journey through life, we are called to follow Jesus. One of the ways we do that is by obeying his command to share the gospel with the world. Our job is to share the good news of Jesus with people, but we can't make anyone believe it. God alone changes people's hearts by his Spirit's work in them so they accept the truth.

God never wastes his, or anyone else's, time. God knows what he is doing with the world he created, and the people he created, far more than we do. Our job is to keep obeying and trusting in him at all times.

25

BETRAYAL

I told them, 'If you think it best, give me my pay; but if not, keep it.' So they paid me thirty pieces of silver.

And the L*ORD* *said to me, 'Throw it to the potter' – the handsome price at which they valued me! So I took the thirty pieces of silver and threw them to the potter at the house of the* L*ORD*. (Zechariah 11:12–13)

Nobody likes rejection; it really hurts. Maybe you've been rejected by a friend and have felt like you've been stabbed in the back. It is never a pleasant feeling. Having invested time in a relationship with someone and enjoyed a period of good friendship and fellowship, being cast aside like you mean nothing is difficult. But, sadly, it does happen.

Rejection and betrayal is not a new thing. In the book of Zechariah, which was written hundreds of years before Jesus was born, we read the story of a leader, a prophet, called Zechariah. This book can be split into two sections, with chapters 1–8 focusing on what happened during his lifetime and chapters 9–14 focusing on what was to come in the future. The future events that Zechariah speaks about have a lot to do with the coming of God's chosen one, the Messiah.

Zechariah 11 is an interesting story of rejection and betrayal. This clearly points us to Jesus and foreshadows Jesus being betrayed by Judas and given over to the Jewish authorities.

Long story short, Zechariah is a shepherd in Israel for a time, but then his relationship with his flock is broken and he resigns. Upon asking for his wages, they offer him a meagre reward – 30 pieces of silver. According to the law in Exodus 21:32, this is the pay-off for a slave who has been injured to the point that they can't work anymore. In other words, the people's payment to Zechariah is a slap in the face. They are saying that he is worthless.

We see history repeating itself when Judas is paid 30 pieces of silver for betraying Jesus. Jesus is God's sent one, the Messiah. He was sent to God's people. Jesus is God's Shepherd. But the people rejected him and instead chose a path of destruction and alienation from God. Judas went to the Jewish authorities and, in similar language to Zechariah, asked for his wages for handing Jesus over. You can see the comparison between Zechariah 11:12 above and Matthew 26:15, where Judas goes to the chief priests and asks, '"What are you willing to give me if I deliver him over to you?" So they counted out for him thirty pieces of silver.'

The betrayal of Jesus was foretold in the Old Testament. The book of Zechariah is a picture of Jesus, God's Messiah, who would come five hundred years later. God's plan to save his people is so precise that even the number of silver coins Judas received were prophesied about hundreds of years before it would happen.

It was part of God's plan that Jesus would be betrayed and handed over to the religious leaders to be killed. That plan was the means by which people are saved today. Jesus knew what would happen to him as Judas met him in the

Garden of Gethsemane and betrayed him with a kiss (Matthew 26:45–50). John 13:21 shows just how hard this betrayal and rejection was for Jesus: 'Jesus was troubled in spirit' when he'd earlier warned his disciples this was going to happen. But Jesus knew the task that was set before him and he paid the price for sins in full so that the Lord's people could be made right with God. Jesus is the true Shepherd who cares for his sheep, and who was betrayed and killed so that we may live.

26

THE CROSS

The LORD said to Moses, 'Make a snake and put it up on a pole; anyone who is bitten can look at it and live.' (Numbers 21:8)

Imagine a courtroom where, instead of real evidence, lies are being told. Imagine a judge who doesn't care whether the accused is innocent or guilty; he just wants him punished. That is so unjust and unfair! But that's the trial that Jesus endured.

After a night of botched legal proceedings, with religious leaders bent on killing Jesus, a large wooden beam was placed on Jesus' back to carry to the place where he would be crucified. But the cross is not merely an act of injustice.

It is also, and more importantly, a battleground where good won the victory over evil.

The crucifixion of Jesus is simultaneously the most tragic and most marvellous event in human history. Tragic because those who shouted for him to be crucified were the same people who, only days before, had been awed by his miracles. They had listened to his teaching and welcomed him into Jerusalem with shouts of praise. But the cross is also marvellous because the whole of the Old Testament had been pointing to this event. It is the moment when Jesus, God in the flesh, would die in the place of sinful humanity so that sinners might live.

The crucifixion was no accident that happened to a good man. Jesus willingly went to the cross knowing that this was all part of God's plan. The cross was the place where forgiveness was made possible for the people of the world. But this scene, with Jesus viciously nailed to an instrument of torture, on display for all to see, should have made those present remember an event from their own history.

In Numbers 21, the people of Israel had already been saved from slavery in Egypt. They were delivered miraculously by God, so there was no doubting that God was on their side. But their confidence didn't last long. Fast forward just a short while and the people had forgotten God's faithfulness and became impatient. They grumbled against God. So the Lord sent venomous snakes into the camp and many people died as a result of their disobedience and rebellion against him. But God was gracious. He told Moses to make a bronze serpent, attach it to a long pole and lift it high in the air. All those who looked at the snake, trusting in God's promise, would be saved and live, but those who did not would die.

This is an important story to remember because we are all infected with the deadliest of poisons: sin. It is a venom that courses through our veins and that results in death, both physically and spiritually. It's the fatal disease that affects every human being. The sin of the world has caused a rift, a breakdown in the relationship between humanity and God. But God has made a way for people to be saved by Jesus dying on the cross in our place. Like the snake was lifted up on the cross , Jesus too was lifted up so that all those who look to him and trust in him are saved from their sin and judgment.

The cross was the place where the Son of God died so that sinful people could live. That's why Christians spend so much time, and dedicate entire books to, talking about the cross. That's why so many Christians wear crosses around their necks. That's why the cross is always part of the good news about Jesus that we share with people. The cross is fundamental to understanding what it means to be a Christian because it was there that Jesus, the innocent one, died in the place of the guilty.

As Jesus hung on the cross, his final words, 'It is finished' (John 19:30), are the most life-giving of all. Three simple words that convey a never-ending promise for all those who trust in Jesus: their punishment before God has been taken. Jesus bore the sin and the shame of the world and traded it for his righteousness, his right standing with God. Jesus made the void, the barrier, between a holy God and an unholy people disappear.

Those final and definitive words of Jesus are just the beginning of new life as a Christian. The separation that was necessary is now no more. The only solution to the problem of sin is Jesus. If we had the cure to a disease that afflicts everyone in the world, we would run out and tell everyone about it. That is why Christians talk so much about Jesus. Everyone in the world needs to know about him.

27

AN END TO SIN

Seventy 'sevens' are decreed for your people and your holy city to finish transgression, to put an end to sin, to atone for wickedness, to bring in everlasting righteousness, to seal up vision and prophecy and to anoint the Most Holy Place. (Daniel 9:24)

Saying sorry isn't always easy. Most of us, in the course of our lives, will have heard a large number of apologies. Some are given freely, for example when a spouse or a colleague realise they've hurt you and are genuinely sorry. Other apologies are not that convincing. For example, a child who took a toy from their little sister and is told to apologise might do so through gritted teeth, with little genuine feeling of remorse.

You have probably apologised for something and then added the common words 'I won't do it again.' However, that isn't always the case. Often we mess up, we get things wrong, we hurt people. Even though our intention is to never do something wrong again, we always do. So the 'sorry cycle' continues.

In the book of Daniel, Daniel prays to God, acknowledging the sin of the people and their lack of commitment to the covenant that they made with him (9:1–19). Daniel acknowledges God's greatness and his consistent faithfulness to the covenant. Daniel ends his prayer with a request for the Lord to deal kindly with his rebellious people and to forgive their sins.

Even as Daniel is still praying, God gives him a message of hope and a glorious future. The Angel Gabriel appears to him and assures Daniel that at the decreed time the Lord's people will repent, say sorry and turn from their sin, and then be forgiven (Daniel 9:24).

Gabriel's message finds its fulfilment in Jesus. Parts of it have already happened; others are still to happen. At the cross, Jesus took the punishment that our sin deserves. He paid the price that others deserve. He willingly subjected himself to death so that his people may be given life. God was gracious to Israel. The people had been warned about their sin; they had been given time to repent. When their Saviour came, at God's appointed time, they did not recognise him. But God's promises of forgiveness and atonement have been fulfilled in the death and resurrection of Jesus.

There are two parts of Daniel 9:24 still to be fulfilled. The 'end to sin' and 'everlasting righteousness' are future promises that will be fulfilled when Jesus returns and brings the everlasting kingdom of God to completion.

The Old Testament helps us to look back and see the fullness of who Jesus is and what he did, but it also points us to the glorious future that awaits his people. I look forward to the day when the 'sorry cycle' doesn't happen anymore because sin has stopped. In that perfect place, called the new creation, sin will be no more and God's people will live in his presence forever. But it's only through Jesus that we can have access to that place. It is only through his death and resurrection that the invitation exists.

Perhaps this is a message you've heard before but never responded to. Today will you listen to the call of Jesus, be forgiven of your sins and join him in that glorious place where sin and pain will be no more?

28

FORGIVENESS

For the life of a creature is in the blood, and I have given it to you to make atonement for yourselves on the altar; it is the blood that makes atonement for one's life. (Leviticus 17:11)

Forgiving people isn't always easy. It can often take time. When we get hurt, it's hard to look past that experience. Friendships aren't always restored right away if someone speaks ill of another. Working relationships aren't always smooth after someone has climbed over you to get one up on the corporate ladder.

As we've already seen in the previous chapters, forgiveness is not just a New Testament idea. In the Old Testament, God taught people that they needed to be forgiven by him and he gave them the sacrificial system as a physical illustration, as Leviticus 17:11 says.

If we find forgiving someone hard after they have hurt us, imagine how hard it would be to forgive them while they are hurting us. Almost impossible, right? Well, that's exactly what Jesus did. In Luke 23:34, while Jesus is hanging nailed to the cross, with his accusers all around him, he says, 'Father, forgive them, for they do not know what they are doing.'

Jesus is asking God to forgive those who are putting him to death. The people, both Jews and Gentiles (non-Jews), are unaware of what they were actually doing. They are ignorant about who Jesus is and what is happening before their eyes. They think that they are killing a rebel, but in fact they are killing the Son of God. However, all of this is under God's absolute control.

The fact that Jesus asks God to forgive his executioners shows us his heart – one of forgiveness and mercy. It also helps us see that forgiveness is open even to his enemies if they repent of their sins and have their eyes opened to the truth of who Jesus is and what he did on the cross.

The same is true for the two criminals crucified with him. Matthew 27:44 tells us that initally both criminals mocked Jesus but Luke 23:40–43 then focuses on one of these men. He defends Jesus' innocence, reprimanding the other for mocking Jesus. Then, in a declaration of faith, he asks to be remembered by Jesus when he enters his kingdom. Jesus responds, 'Truly I tell you, today you will be with me in paradise' (verse 43).

Jesus forgives a man who mocked him. Jesus asks for forgiveness to be offered to those who, in ignorance, are killing him. Thank the Lord that Jesus' heart is full of forgiveness and mercy for the sinner because this is what has enabled the offer of forgiveness to ring down through the ages. It is because of Jesus' heart and God's plan for salvation that Christians today can be sure of their forgiveness. It is through Jesus' obedience to God's plan, his death and his resurrection that our forgiveness is even possible.

Thankfully, Jesus is more gracious and forgiving than we are. While we sometimes find it hard to forgive those who have hurt us, God saw fit to send his Son to a people who he knew would reject and kill him. But, on top of that, Jesus' forgiveness is far greater than our own, because his is eternal and restores our relationship with God. Forgiveness from God is not temporary, nor is it given reluctantly. It is given freely to those who repent and believe in Jesus' death on their behalf. True forgiveness is the call from a holy God to a rebellious and unholy people to come and follow him.

29

THE GRAVE

Now the Lord *provided a huge fish to swallow Jonah, and Jonah was in the belly of the fish three days and three nights.* (Jonah 1:17)

There are some parts of the Old Testament that very clearly point forward to Jesus, with the connection easy to find and quite explicit. But there are other stories where the link may be harder to draw out. Sometimes this work is already done on our behalf. The New Testament picks up on some Old Testament events or themes and helps us to see how they relate to and are fulfilled in Jesus. An example is the story of Jonah, which many people know.

Jonah is a prophet, a spokesperson for God. He is asked to go to an enemy city called Nineveh and tell the people to repent – an intimidating task because the Ninevites are scary. Jonah doesn't want these enemies to receive God's forgiveness and so he runs away from God and jumps on a boat heading in the opposite direction. When God sends a storm, this results in Jonah being thrown overboard and then being swallowed by a big fish. Three days later, Jonah is vomited onto dry land and eventually does what God had asked him to do by going to Nineveh.

You're probably thinking, 'How on earth does that point to Jesus?' Well, in Mathew 12:38–41, the Pharisees – the religious elite of Jesus' day – ask for a sign to prove who Jesus is. Jesus responds, 'A wicked and adulterous generation asks for a sign!' (verse 39). Here 'wicked' means that their hearts struggle to see the truth, and they are 'adulterous' because though they should be faithful to God, they are on the lookout for other desirable things.

Jesus continues on to say that the only sign that will be given to them is the sign of Jonah. Just as Jonah was in the belly of the big fish before miraculously reappearing, so during the three days of Easter, Jesus died, was buried and lay in a tomb before rising again. The sign that will be made clear to the Pharisees is that Jesus is the greater Jonah. He won't be vomited from a fish but will rise triumphant from the grave, defeating death and sin.

The Pharisees attribute Jesus' miracles to demonic work, but his resurrection from the dead will be a clear sign of his identity as the Son of God. They won't be able to deny it. Jonah was a prophet and a preacher who took God's Word to a rebellious people and called them to repent. Jesus is the ultimate prophet sent by God because he himself is God. He is the greatest preacher, who calls people to repent and believe 'for the kingdom of God has come near' (Matthew 4:17). But more than that, Jesus is the Saviour. Only he, through his death and resurrection, has made salvation and peace with God possible again.

We too, like the Pharisees, are a wicked and adulterous people. Our hearts are always being pulled in different directions, looking for new things to worship and love. But like the Israelites had been given the sign of Jonah, we have been given the resurrection of Jesus as a sign pointing to Jesus' true identity. If it really happened, and I'm convinced that it did, then it becomes clear that Jesus was not just a man or a teacher, but is in fact the Saviour of the world.

30

THE RESURRECTION

I know that my redeemer lives,
and that in the end he will
stand on the earth.
And after my skin has been destroyed,
yet in my flesh I will see God;
I myself will see him
with my own eyes – I, and not another.
How my heart yearns within me!
(Job 19:25–27)

If Jesus' resurrection didn't actually happen, then Christianity falls apart. If the resurrection is false, then all Christians are to be pitied and the Christian faith is useless (1 Corinthians 15:12–19). The good news is that Jesus did rise from the dead!

But we also look forward to a future resurrection – the resurrection of all people. On the final day, Christians will be raised to life in Jesus, while those who have rejected Jesus will be raised to face the judgment of God.

The resurrection is a theme that runs throughout the whole Bible because it is glorious and because it brings hope.

It is glorious for those with faith in Jesus because it means that we will be in perfect harmony with God. There will be no pain, no suffering and no sin. The pictures the Bible gives us about our future eternity with God are beautiful. We will be in a place that at present we cannot begin to fully comprehend – a place of beauty; a place of work, without that labour being hard; a place of harmony with God and with our fellow Christians. We will be living the perfect life that we were created to live. The resurrection will be glorious. Therefore, the resurrection also gives us hope.

In one of the oldest books of the Old Testament, we meet Job. Job was a man who knew suffering. His family were killed, his livelihood was taken away, he went from being well-known and loved to being a mess on a rubbish heap. His was quite literally a riches-to-rags story. But in the midst of Job's suffering, he holds firm to a promise, one of the earliest in the Bible, – that of Job 19:25–27.

Even in the midst of great suffering, Job finds hope in a future with God. His confidence that one day he will see his redeemer brings him comfort. However, he only knew part of the story. He had no idea about Jesus, and how Jesus would live, die and be raised to life again. Job didn't know the message that Jesus would preach about the kingdom of God and the assurance he would give his followers that if they came to him, they would find true and everlasting rest.

But standing on this side of the cross, we have a greater view of our future resurrection than Job ever did. In the Bible, Jesus' teaching has been revealed to us. Descriptions of our eternal future have been shown to us in part. The curtain has been peeled back slightly to reveal the glories of eternal life with God, which produces in us a hope and an eager yearning for that day to come quicker.

For the Christian, that day of resurrection – that day of joy everlasting – is a certainty through Jesus. Let the glory and hope of eternity fuel your praise of God today. Let the promise of the new creation lift your eyes to see the wonder of the gospel. Let it stir in you a heart of praise that is directed to our wonderful God who made salvation possible through Jesus Christ and who has opened our eyes to this truth by his Holy Spirit.

31

THE EMMAUS ROAD

> *Now that same day two of them were going to a village called Emmaus, about seven miles from Jerusalem. They were talking with each other about everything that had happened. As they talked and discussed these things with each other, Jesus himself came up and walked along with them; but they were kept from recognising him.* (Luke 24:13–16)

Let's take a step back. We've journeyed through some of the key Old Testament events and passages that point forward to Jesus. These may be what Jesus uses to explain to Cleopas and the other follower travelling along the road how all of the Old Testament points to him.

Imagine how they are feeling. Their teacher has been crucified. They have lost a friend. They are probably confused about everything and possibly thinking whether it was all for nothing.

But Jesus comes alongside them and helps them understand everything that has happened. In the following chapters of this book, we'll turn our attention to the final verses in Luke 24. We'll see what our response should be, having journeyed through the Old Testament and understood more about Jesus' life, death and resurrection.

It is not enough if our knowledge about Jesus only informs our minds; it should transform our lives. Therefore, in the final part of Luke 24, Jesus appears to Cleopas and his friend along with the disciples and gives them instructions of what that transformation should look like.

I hope, as you've read this book, you've been able to see that Jesus wasn't just a good man or a competent communicator. Jesus is God in the flesh, and that should impact our lives and encourage us to live for him.

PART 3:

THE JOURNEY CONTINUES

32

SPREADING THE STORY

Then they worshipped him and returned to Jerusalem with great joy. And they stayed continually at the temple, praising God.
(Luke 24:52–53)

The story of Jesus has changed the world over the last two thousand years. From Luke 24 onwards, we see an exponential growth. At first, the disciples stay in Jerusalem, praising God. Then, in the book of Acts – the account of the beginning of the early church – the disciples spread the good news of Jesus. The pattern that we see in Acts is that the gospel grows as it is opposed. Throughout church history, the same has been true. As people and empires have stood against the good news of Jesus, all they have done is to further the work of God's Word rather than hinder it. God's Word will always be proclaimed through ordinary people enabled by God's Spirit.

Many of the disciples were fishermen – a few ordinary people who spent time with Jesus. Their message initially spread through persecution. As Christians were dispersed, they took the gospel with them – they could not hide it from the world. Imagine you had the greatest news in the world to share – a message of true and lasting hope, a message of forgiveness and eternal happiness. You wouldn't dream of keeping it to yourself!

That's what we have in Jesus. He lived the perfect life of obedience that we never could. He died the death that we all deserve, bearing the full weight of God's wrath. He rose triumphant from the grave, defeating sin and death. That simple message changed the lives of the disciples and the early church. It changes lives today too, and every Christian is a testimony of that.

The good news of Jesus is not just wishful thinking. It's not just a nice story to keep us going. The good news of Jesus is a real story that has changed lives, countries and cultures. The goal was never for the church to be a separate people who retreat into a holy huddle and only focus on themselves. The church's goal has always been to flood the world with the message of Jesus so that every ear hears his name and is able to understand the gospel. That hasn't yet happened. We're still involved in the task of spreading the story of Jesus.

There are an estimated 7.9 billion people on this planet, with approximately 385,000 babies being born every day. 3.27 billion of the world's population are classed as unreached, meaning that they have little or no knowledge of Jesus or the Bible. 42.5% of the world's population doesn't know much about Jesus.

The church has come a long way in two thousand years. It started with 12 disciples. Acts 1:15 describes a group that had become about 120 followers of Jesus. Now, there's estimated to be over two billion Christians worldwide. Yet there are still so many who are unreached. This story has not yet finished spreading, and we have a role to play in that. We are called to repent of our sins and trust in Jesus, then we are told to share the gospel freely for all to hear. Their response is in the Lord's hands, but our responsibility is to go.

Think of just three people with whom you could share the gospel. Pray that God would open their hearts so that they too would join the church. Then continue to witness to Jesus and spread his story across the globe.

33

OUR EQUIPMENT

> *I am going to send you what my Father has promised; but stay in the city until you have been clothed with power from on high.* (Luke 24:49)

I moved house recently, so I've got used to putting pieces of furniture together. Flatpack furniture is great, provided you have (and use!) all the right tools and equipment. Imagine being tasked to build a bed, but not following the instructions and not using the correct tools. Most likely, your bed would look quite different from what you thought you were putting together.

Perhaps you read the previous chapter and, considering the task that Christians have been given of sharing Jesus with the world, found it daunting. But Christians are not doing this job alone. We have been given both instructions in the Bible and all the equipping that we need by God's Spirit – that 'power from on high'. Jesus is talking here about the Holy Spirit.

While Jesus was on earth, he promised his disciples that he would send the Holy Spirit (John 14:15–27). The Holy Spirit would teach the disciples and remind them of Jesus' words (verse 26). Turning to the book of Acts, we see the arrival of the Holy Spirit, who came in power and enabled the spread of the gospel, starting in Jerusalem.

The same Holy Spirit who came in power in Acts 2, and who worked in the lives of the 12 disciples and the early church to spread the gospel with power and conviction, is in every Christian today. We have not been called to go to the world in our own strength. We have power from on high, through the Holy Spirit, to boldly go and speak about Jesus in the world.

The Holy Spirit equips and gifts the Lord's people to do his work. There are countless stories throughout history of Christians who have changed the lives of so many people because the Holy Spirit has enabled and equipped them to do so. Some of those people are remembered, but many of them lived, died and have been forgotten by the world.

The task of every Christian is to live a life worthy of the Lord's calling, to go out equipped by the Spirit and to tell the world about Jesus. Our job is not to be remembered or to make a name for ourselves. Our job is to glorify Jesus and make him famous while we serve him wholeheartedly.

Start to share the good news about Jesus with your family, your friends, your neighbours and your colleagues. Pray that the Holy Spirit would give you opportunities to tell them about Jesus and for the boldness to take those opportunities. We have been given a task, but we've also been given the power to fulfil that task by the Holy Spirit.

Maybe, as you draw near the end of this book, you're still unsure about what you believe about Jesus. If you want to find out more, you could pray that God would open your eyes to see the truth about Jesus. Ask the Holy Spirit to equip you to see Jesus for who he is – God in the flesh.

34

JESUS' ASCENSION

When he had led them out to the vicinity of Bethany, he lifted up his hands and blessed them. While he was blessing them, he left them and was taken up into heaven. (Luke 24:50–51)

In the Old Testament, when a king returned from winning a battle, there would be a victory procession in the city. The victorious king would ascend to his throne, proving his triumph, and would receive gifts from his subjects for his efforts.

In contrast, when the Lord rescued his people from Egypt by defeating their enemies (the Egyptians) and bringing them through the wilderness, he gave them his law. This partly told the Israelites how he, a holy God, could dwell with an unholy people.

We have here two different images of a victorious king. One wins and receives, while the other wins and gives.

In Ephesians 4:8, Paul quotes from Psalm 68:18: 'When he ascended on high, he took many captives and gave gifts to his people.' Psalm 68 is a call for God to come and rescue his people, and uses imagery of God returning to the city of Jerusalem like a victorious king returning from battle. Paul connects this verse to Jesus and his ascension. Paul's main point is that Jesus was raised from the dead and has returned to heaven, ascending to the right hand of God the Father. As a victorious King, Jesus gives gifts to his people. Jesus has gifted us the founders of the church – the apostles. Jesus also gives the church different people, all equipped to build up the church with his Word, the Bible. Each 'office' mentioned in Ephesians 4:11 – 'the apostles, the prophets, the evangelists, the pastors and teachers' – is there to equip Christians in the church to grow to full maturity in the faith (verses 12–13).

Paul uses the analogy of the church being a body, with its different parts each having an important role to play. Jesus is the head of that body. All things hold together through Jesus. We should be a body that is built up and ready for the return of Jesus, the head.

Jesus ascending into heaven in Luke 24:50–53 is therefore important because it shows us that Jesus is victorious over sin and death, and that he has given us gifts to enable us to be the church and people that we are called to be. Our response as we read about Jesus' ascension should be the same as the first disciples: we should worship him with great joy (verse 52).

The ascension of Jesus also shows us his divine nature; he is in glory with the Father, interceding on behalf of his people. In addition, his ascension points forward to the glorious day when Jesus will return. When Jesus ascended into heaven, angels promised that Jesus would return as the disciples saw him leave (Acts 1:11). Until that day comes, the ascended and victorious King Jesus has given his body, the church, a job – to take the good news of Jesus to the world.

35

THE END GOAL OF THE STORY

Then I saw 'a new heaven and a new earth,' for the first heaven and the first earth had passed away, and there was no longer any sea. I saw the Holy City, the new Jerusalem, coming down out of heaven from God, prepared as a bride beautifully dressed for her husband. And I heard a loud voice from the throne saying, 'Look! God's dwelling-place is now among the people, and he will dwell with them. They will be his people, and God himself will be with them and be their God. "He will wipe every tear from their eyes. There will be no more death" or mourning or crying or pain, for the old order of things has passed away.' (Revelation 21:1–4)

Every good story has a good ending. Tension builds throughout the story, growing and growing until at last the problems are satisfyingly resolved. A hero arises and a battle rages, until finally, the happy ending. Hollywood is built on this pattern of storytelling: Frodo destroys the ring; the White Witch is defeated. Battles are fought in which the goodies win and the baddies lose.

Picture yourself again with the two followers on the road to Emmaus (Luke 24:13–35). As Jesus walks with them, explaining the Scriptures, they reach their destination. The two stop at a house and invite Jesus to stay with them. At dinner, when Jesus breaks the bread and gives it to them, their eyes are opened. They realise who he is. But suddenly he disappears.

They rush back to the others to tell them all that has happened. Jesus then appears to the whole group, blesses them and later ascends to heaven. Jesus had prepared his disciples and followers throughout his whole public ministry for this day – the day when he would leave them.

Eternal life is not only something in the future; there are many blessings that Christians today enjoy in Jesus. However, the end of the gospel story is the eternal future that awaits Christians in the new creation.

Popular ideas of heaven include little babies with wings and playing harps while floating on clouds. But the new creation is described in physical terms. The earth will be remade without the effects of sin. We will dwell with God and there will be some element of work involved.

While there are plenty of things that we do not fully understand about this new creation, we know enough. There will be no more sin, pain or suffering, and God will live with his people, who will enjoy him forever. In Revelation 21:1–4, we see this new creation and the glorious end of the story. While we are all still longing for this, learn more about it. Grow with eager anticipation of that day when God will live with his people forever.

36

WHERE DO YOU FIT INTO THIS STORY?

The story of Jesus didn't start when he was born in Bethlehem many years ago. It has been unfolding from the very beginning of the world. The Old Testament is fulfilled in Jesus, who revealed God to the world. We now have the whole Bible, which tells us about him.

But the story of Jesus doesn't stop at the end of the Bible either; it continues today. As Christians share the truth about Jesus with the world, and as people put their trust in him and are forgiven, the story continues and grows. As the church of Christ is built, as missionaries travel to distant shores and as Christians reach their neighbours next door, more and more chapters are added to this cosmic saga.

The question that remains is: where do you fit in this story? Jesus has made it possible for sinners to be forgiven and transformed, to be made right with God. Jesus has called and enabled his people to live distinctive lives that demonstrate the gospel in everyday life. Jesus has empowered and equipped his church to be ambassadors of the good news.

Perhaps you're struggling to live a distinctive life for Jesus. We will all fail at times, but he has given you all the power that you need to be faithful (2 Peter 1:3–4) and has promised to be with you until the end (Matthew 28:20). Jesus knows your struggles, temptations and fears (Hebrews 4:15), but despite all that he wants you as part of his story. Keep following him!

Maybe you're still feeling new to all this or you've never thought about it before and have more questions. If so, I would suggest reading the Gospel of Mark to learn about what Jesus said and did while he was on earth. But perhaps you're ready to take the step of following Jesus for the first time. He invites you today to become his follower and play your part in his story.

If you would like to trust in Jesus for the first time, you could pray with words like this:

Dear God,

Thank you that you sent your Son Jesus into the world to live the perfect life that I never could and to die the death that I deserve under the weight and judgment of sin. Thank you that Jesus did not stay in the grave but rose triumphant, defeating sin and death and making a relationship with you possible. By your Holy Spirit, I ask you to come into my life, forgive me of my sins and help me follow Jesus. I pray in the name of Jesus,

Amen.

The Bible assures you that 'If you declare with your mouth, "Jesus is Lord," and believe in your heart that God raised him from the dead, you will be saved' (Romans 10:9).

If you have become a Christian, telling another believer about it is a great idea. They can celebrate with you and help you as you begin following Jesus.

The conversation on the Emmaus Road transformed Cleopas and his friend that first Easter Sunday. When they finally understood who had walked with them towards home, they couldn't contain their joy. 'They asked each other, "Were not our hearts burning within us while he talked with us on the road and opened the Scriptures to us?"' (Luke 24:32). Whether you have just become a Christian or have been following Jesus for a while, my prayer is that as you walk through life with Jesus, you will continue exploring the whole of the Bible, and that you heart would also burn within you as you see him more and more on every page.

essentials
the heart of the Christian faith
LEE MCMUNN
'a remarkable little book . . . for all who long to understand Jesus more deeply.' – Michael Card
THE LITTLE HIM BOOK
OOKING AT THE JESUS WHO MAKES OUR HEARTS SING
PETER MEAD
Unlocking
Mark's Gospel
31 keys to help you read the Bible
Ruth Bridcut